Still Swingin'

ALSO IN THE BLACKWORDS™ POETRY SERIES
Jazz Poetry Kafe: The BlackWords Compilation CD (Various Artists)
Kupenda: Love Poems by Kwame Alexander
These Hips by Tonya M. Matthews
360° A Revolution of Black Poets edited by Salaam with Alexander
Real Soul Food & other poetic recipes by Stacey Evans Morgan
Just Us: poems and counterpoems, 1986-1995 by Kwame Alexander

Still Swingin' These Hips

Tonya Maria Matthews

BlackWords

BlackWords Poetry Series
Published by BlackWords Press
PO Box 21, Alexandria, VA 22313
www.blackwordsonline.com

BlackWords and the portrayal of the Fist with the
Pencil are trademarks of BlackWords, Inc.

Publisher: Stephanie Stanley Alexander
Senior Publishing Consultant: Kwame Alexander
Book & Cover Design: www.dothewritething.net

ISBN 1-888018-17-8

Some of these poems have previously appeared in
"These Hips & other Songs to Minista to a
people's soul," Horizongmag.com,
and Prometheus Black.

Cover Artwork "The Palm Wine Tapper II"
By Uche Ukoh

First Edition: January 2002
Printed in the United States of America
1 3 5 7 9 10 8 6 4 2

Publishers and Producers
of Fine Black Literature & Performance

Dedicated to My Mother, who constantly told her daughter to "modulate your voice," but never shut up...

Contents

SWING SWING SWING

ACKNOWLEDGEMENTS

Foreword

Numbers, like age, can be deceiving.

It was pre-Christmas 1999. The year was ending, and wasn't too much poetry happening in Chocolate City. Light bulbs went on in my head. So, I called a few friends, put an ad in the paper, sent out an email, and held a poetry slam on a stormy Saturday night. The prize was $50. The room was empty. Probably fifteen people showed up. *And half of them were poets.*

Each approached the Mic with a timid walk and equally timid delivery. This was turning out to be a pretty boring piece of entertainment I had coordinated. We neared the final two poets, and I was eager to get home and catch The Pretender while complaining about how poets in DC don't support each other.

And then she walked in.

Well, not really walked, more like some ancient Egyptian combination of sashaying and sauntering. I mean she catwalked like a "runway angel on a Parisian nightcloud." Walked right up to the Mic like she owned it—like she was next. Actually, she was, as she was so *together* she had "pre-registered" for the slam, and I was about to call her name.

And then she said something.

Well, not really said something, more like spoke something, screamed something, straight sang something… about 'these hips'
about 'fallen soldiers'
about you
about me
about us.
And we 15 were floored, suddenly glad that we had ventured out in the dark rain to this even darker jazz club in Northwest

DC. Thankful that numbers can sometimes be deceiving.

Two years ago, I learned age ain't nothin' but two digits on your drivers license, as this twenty-three year old diva renewed my faith in words. That night, she handily won the $50, and my dedication. I became an instant supporter, an eager dreamcometruemaker. "You want to publish a book, I asked her." Trying not to sound too excited for fear of confusing my entrepreneurial enthusiasm with flirtation, I responded to her affirmative with "Well, if you are serious, then get me the book in a few weeks, and we can publish a chapbook within the month." It wasn't impossible, but it was very close. Then again, I didn't expect her or any other poet to be that "serious."

A week later, she called. Wanted to get my mailing address.

Two years later, I am more in awe of her as I was then. She is the embodiment of a serious performer and a writer. Make no mistake she is still fine-tuning her voice, still learning, still growing, and still swingin…And we, her readers, are lucky to be along on this leg of her journey. This collection of new and old poems is a testament to her knowledge and love of poetry and life.

At our first meeting, I recall asking her about future plans. She indicated that she was a full-time graduate student, working on a Ph.D. in Biomedical Engineering at Johns Hopkins. The next thing out her mouth threw me. "I want to have something to fall back on in case the poetry doesn't work out."

No chance of that happening, Tonya!

—*Kwame Alexander*

2

Still Swingin'
These Hips

THESE HIPS

These hips are wide as hell.
Curving and growing and bursting
With the tales they tell.
Wide enough to balance heavy chests and square
 shoulders into characteristically plump hourglass
figures.
Wide enough to stop crap games on
shady ghetto corners.
Wide enough to birth fat black baby boys.

These hips are wide as hell.
Heaving and stretching and yearning
Masses of cocoa-tinted mocha-touched caramel-licked
flesh
Working far into the midnight hour.
Wide enough
 — ooh baby! baby! —
to accentuate curvaceous backsides that beget
 outlandish hip-hop hits.
Wide enough to cradle you, baby love, after hours
 on a job.
that chastises your skin, devalues your mind and
 scars your soul.
Wide enough for hours of painstaking,
 labor-of-love cornrows for you, baby girl.

These hips are wide as hell.
Leaning and locking and swiveling
Helping my mouth articulate what words simply
 cannot handle.
Wide enough to manipulate my walk into a graceful
 or attitudinal

— but always incomparable —
Sway that defines who I am
Today.
Wide enough to remind you of the error of your ways,
black man:
remind you that you like a woman you can hold onto.
Wide enough to cradle you, grandbaby,
 when your momma cries on my shoulder
 because this time daddy is gone for good.

These hips, these hips.
They are for me.
They are for me.
They are for me.
They are for you.
They are for you.
They are for you.
They are for definition, for comfort
for sex appeal, for motherhood
for play, for work
for weekends, for everyday
for tight dresses, for A-line skirts
for politics, for protest
for war, for worship.
For me.
For you.
For real.
These hips, my hips
are wide as hell.

Swing proud enough to remember where you come from. Swing proud enough to remember your name…

SWING PROUD

I

"I believe in pride of race and lineage and self; in pride of self so deep as to scorn injustice to other selves" – *W. E. B. DuBois*

Nikki's Daughter

in a time past
my yawn was tsunami
pushing the dark man past honshu
and into harlem
shango dared imply that
in this i had erred
false gods make mistakes
i make plans
so i sneezed and
pearls dripped out of my nose
became langston and zora
and duke and billie and
freedom

yes i am *she*
that tough tight omnipotent
bold   cold
wind chill factor 360 degrees above
false identity
mass media cannot camouflage
the destiny of
nikki's daughter

the constellations are my autobiography
you still don't know me
still can't know me
my lover and i made nations
conquered universes and
created revolution
but even he
only knows my second middle name

make no mistake
i am not the moon
flattered
you mistook me for one so young
i am she who took match
and lit the sun
i am fierce
i am lion
i am civilization
there are days when
i just   *am*

so good
my crimes are cardinal virtues
so bad
i am the reason the devil needs an advocate
i am temptation
the first man tried to taste of me
and hell was created when i told him
he couldn't have any more

i danced before there were drummers
i am rhythm
i ate before there was food
i am bounty
i drink of oceans and feast upon stray planets
so magnificient
my excretions can be seen from satellites
the Nile is my number one
the Himalayas, my number two

long ago traveling this earth
my walking stick cut out the grand canyon
my dropped earring became the first egyptian pyramid
my discarded chastity belt, the great barrier reef
i created laughter with a wink

and melody with a hiccup
while my teardrops melted into butterflies
before this world ever knew sadness

the wind is nothing more than breath
left over from lullabies i sing
to my seventh son
on the seventh day of the seventh month
in the seventh year of his life
he will defeat the beast of triple imperfection
and hang africa around my neck in commemoration
it will be my best birthday ever

do not marvel
at this mere trickle of my great water
there is more to come, for
i, too, will have
a daughter.

Chickenhead

(*Ungiven Rights Remix*)
The next time you call me
chickenhead

I might have to hurt you.
If you feel the need to call me out my name
try   Nefertiti
            Cleopatra
hell, baby, call me Eve
but don't call me chickenhead.

Boo...
...I don't cluck.
That bock bock baaaaack! sound you hear
just wisdom bouncing off your virgin eardrums.

I.
Don't.
Cluck.
Chickens cluck.
Don't call me a chickenhead.

Sweet thang...
...I fly.
My soul soars, my spirit leaps to keep up.
Yesterday my heart sprouted wings and
my mind is always in flight.

Chickens.
Don't.
Fly.
I do. So
don't call me a chickenhead.

Honey pie...
...I don't lay eggs.
Ahemm.
I said
I don't lay eggs.
I make nations.
You did not pick your way out of cold white shell
fight to be free from solitary encapsulation
your only comfort, nourishment
yellow, yolky mass.
You rested in warmth of my womb
took comfort in my lullaby
ate my food.

Man-boy, remember this the last time
I tell you...

...baby brown sugar daddy sweet, my beloved
cuddlebug...
if you want to call me out my name
try   Queen
                Oshun
On good days call me Goddess
but don't
dare
call me

chickenhead.

skill

(for bell hooks' grandmother)
people had to die
before we got jobs
little beady-eyed white men
with big, black mustaches
kept multiplying
started winning
and they needed me
and her and her and she
to make more guns
more cannons
more ways to kill more
beady-eyed white men
with big, black mustaches
in the end
they wanted their jobs back
they wanted us back
where we'd been kept before
but by then, remember,
we knew how to make guns

Diva Divine

Search for a queen
find crowns and the smiles attached to them.
become the enemy in an effort to teach
rejection of fed heart and free mind.
Things would be so much better if we remember the
word
    diva
the same root as
    divine.
Throw away the good with the bad
dismiss dreams you never had
disregard your possibilities like an old deck of cards
de-clare-war
on definitions of civilization as you know it
contemplate notions of civilization as originally built
in your mind/

/you are diva divine/

/barefoot and pregnant with information
to build nation
change this world for little girls
transform derogatory cliché into words you need to say
to start a riot

Pregnant and barefoot
cuz you don't need shoes for walking across battlefields
for starting revolutions.
Absolution is option for few.
Perfunctory prayers will not save you.
Save *you*. Claim you. When you/

/recognize diva divine/

/in yourself
resisting categorization like vegetables on a shelf

example:
Since his greenbacks stole her from another
He'd dismiss sis as regula skeeza
psychologically batter his soulmate
into being with his best man
dancing at his best club
said I'll love you more
if you let me watch but
lap dance may be last dance
if sistah has got scissors in her crotch

Unquietly kept
you already been told
ain't no such thing as an ordinary ho.
One time too many
abusing sistahs of the street
next time you ask Who shot ya?
answer might be She
with pistol as pretty as eyes are fine/

/beware diva divine/

/your greatest mistake
rewarded with greatest miracle.
Accept this gift of life
though your youth the cost
God's grace
Satan's loss
To be a mother is divine.
Create in your own image, queen
forsake the modest

no shame in your game
raise your daughter diva and goddess

all things changed
ideals rearranged
sins remitted
heart committed
wounds healed in time

/resurrect diva divine/

Like the wooden trays of Ife
we say your success is predetermined
your demise, imminent.
Keep climbing 40 steps of ladder
lest your position on the bottom rung become
permanent, unchangeable

Rearrangeable destinies mark the path of every sistah
sojourning
for the truth, the learning
easy to memorize.
Store wisdom in your eyes
hypnotize your own worst enemy
until reflection makes ultimate confession
    self-doubt, snuff out like fire's forgotten ember
    take heed, remember
Third eye open, vision granted
    You shall see Jah.

Rejoice!

divine diva.

(H)our Glass Figures

Trace these curves with your fingertips.
Etch this infinite shape forever in the minds of a
people
destined to forget their own mother.

Our glass figures resist shattering
though they aim with
sharp words sharpened
on the grindstones of mistruth and myth and mammy
mindless miseducated men of all breeds
treating darker woman as half-breed
bred for this harlotry that began with slavery
but didn't end with it...

Hourglass figure.
You figure me your plaything.
You play with me? Me play with you?
I play with seeds when I'm building my nation
with spears when they threaten my children
with pistols when they hang my man.
I don't have time to play with you.
African lives on western shores are not a game.

Want to trace these curves with your fingertips
carve hourglass figures into sultry shadows
draw us black in the nighttime
but draw us black
when the day comes and we are still black
with these hourglass figures we cannot pass
as anything less than mother
of a nation.

Draw us black in the daytime
for when the light comes we are still black
with these hourglass figures we cannot pass
the time in silence.
Sands slip like tears through this hourglass
in an hour, I guess,
this world will come to an end
figure-atively speaking, of course
but our course is charted through Armageddon
because our glass figures are molded
    in apocalyptic flame
our glass figures will not crack
    under the pressures of new beginnings
our glass figures are hand blown
by the great I Am   We Are as infinite
as the shape we bear.

Hourglass figure.
So I figure I have the shape of utility
child on this hip, sword on that one
chopping down all weeds who threaten my baby's path.

Hourglass figure.
So I figure as time starts anew
I'll flip myself over and this whole world, too
only you who cling to these proper roots
can continue to hang
as my sands wash through
while goddess cuts loose lost souls
reverse rotates this planet
starts all life anew.

If your minds are as quick as my sands
I might just let you trace these curves
    with your fingertips
etch this infinite shape into your mind...
    ...people
don't forget your mother.

Swing wide enough to catch all who have fallen and all who have gone astray and all who tire in the fight...

SWING WIDE

"For I am my mother's daughter, and the drums of Africa still beat in my heart. They will not let me rest while there is still a single Negro boy or girl without a chance to prove his worth"
–*Mary McLeod Bethune*

Blood Spangled Banner

O say can you seeeeeee
that our parents fought for our right called privilege
to live this American Dream
but we're using said freedoms to
map out this country's most popular nightmare.See
a nation ain't a nation
if we can't give rise to a younger generation and
we won't get no younger generation if
all the child-bearing-aged kids is dead. Instead of
continuing these battles
to better our society
we choose to wed standards of mediocrity.
Wanna laugh at White boys
for playing chicken with a bus –
cuz of some movie they saw
think that game requires more skill than luck, but
listen to the radio and think it's perfectly sane
for all my real live niggas to
throw their
gats
up?

What so proudly we hailed
all the rappers who have fallen
For justice I'm still callin
while ignorant ones keep hollerin
bout places saved in heaven for thee
by the Notorious B.I.G. but
just cuz he rapped about carrying a piece
don't mean he made one with his God.

Ain't it odd?

Folks spend more time tryin to earn respect
than a seat on the right side for judgment day.
Quiet as it's kept
you going bout both the wrong way
slain human beings become hip-hop cliché
and I say:
Peace out to L.L. Cool J.
but CanIBust this rhyme?
The notorious G. O. D.
is the greatest rapper of all time.
Verses have been remixed redubbed revamped
more times than Christians care to think about
but for all your sampled visions   numerical
references
still walkin in a cloud of doubt.

All Tupac needed to pack was
mo wisdom, less attitude.
Gon leave his home town
go across the country
then start actin rude.
Perpin in a foreign land
     like you wearing a full metal jacket.
Is your mind been over-blown?Have
you become a victim of your own press packet?
Thinking you can hang with the criminals
cuz you got real hardcore raps
but now the only song you samplin, son

Taps.

It's gettin hard to break these chains
in the land of the   free.
Starting to look more like
the home of theeee...

Don't make me say it.
White folks abolished slavery in the 1850's
kicked it around till the 1960's
now Black folks wanna bring it back in the 2G?
I'm now in a land
where the pimps
have become producers
    the prostitutes divas.
Where does that leave us?

Our parents turn to grieve us as they
look into my eyes and
see this dead girl walkin
Tired of all this bull-talking bout
revolution
claiming it won't be televised
but the television is where you keep your eyes
glued to all the scantily clad tricks and
their shaking thighs.
hollering wit yo boys:
"Ooo. That phat bitch! Know I'd fuck her!"
Flip the script, turn it around
that bitch could be your sistah, mistah.

Instead of lyrical play
you literally slay your rival
cops clocking that's okay
figure you'll sell more records underground.Oops!
looked up and
your white record distributor
no longer anywhere to be found.

So much money filling pockets of hip-hop   industry
ain't got time place rhyme reason to see
    Benjamin Franklin's

laughin at yo ass
every time that record goes gold.See
to sell that many copies
you first had to sell your soul.
Trading rocket's red glare for gloc's white flashes
you only out for self
but to do this you must destroy the masses?
Turning my national anthem
    into blood spangled banner...

hold up
this shout ain't just going out to hip-hop performer.
Nawh, high roller
not just coming at you
cuz the brother that listens to his CD player
more than his own momma
is a *special kind of fool*.

Take off those headphones
turn down that track.Fact
there's a whole lot more to being black
than this gun-slinging servitude and financial slavery.
Memorize lessons unlearned
    by our fallen hip-hopera soldiers
ignore all of this
post
mortem
hype.
There really are six million ways to die brutha

CHOOSE LIFE.

Trivial Pursuits

I.

Sometimes I've got to remind myself
that all this shit
is just trivial.
Like it's trivial when some man propositions me
on my way to church, mistaking me for
overdressed hooker
or still even more trivial
when he then turns to proposition my little sister
cuz he's just that kind of a freak.

Another network paying demoralized
— or perhaps just starving —
black actors millions of dollars
to do millenium remix of the 30's bull
shuckin' and jivin' shuckin' and jivin' shuckin' and
jivin'
70 years later it is still shucking and jiving.
Just trivial.
In fact a small black man
not a big white one
thought that idea up. Trivial.

II.

Another black child
and another and another
dies. Shot to death.
News at Six
Seven
Ten
Ten-thirty and
Eleven.

Trivial.

The first shot by a friend. Trivial.
Second shot by accident. Trivial.
The third?
Shot by a cop
born in his own hood
raised on his own block
babysat by his own mamma
got lucky
got out
got forgotten
then began to forget.
When he got the radio call
he came right in
guns blazing
no "stop"
no "halt"
no love.
Shot his former neighbor in the back
a case of mistaken identity
justified use of force
though he owes that dead kid
two G.I. Joes and a Tonka Truck
for a traded Jackie Robinson baseball card.

It's all just
trivial
like
crack

pipes, heads, babies.

Babies giving head to stop the headaches they have
from the heartache they fear of going another day
without love
without mama
without money
without respect
without rent
without hope
without the babies they bore
but the help services took away. Trivial.

Trivial like
how her new boss put his hands on sistah girl. Trivial.
Laughed and snarled when she said she'd sue
"Why the hell else would we hire a nigger bitch like
you?"

Trivial like
how bruh man got fired.
— back on the streets could be toting a gun —
Mad as hell cuz he caught the rap
for the missing 50 bucks
was in the pocket of the owner's son. Trivial.

III.

Trivial the NAACP is suspected of fraud.
Trivial the Nation is suspected of murder.
Trivial Martin's dead and Clarence is still alive.
Trivial HBCUs are closing down and HWCUs don't
wanna let us in.
Trivial Betty was burning alive when Marge Schott
should be burning in hell.
Trivial rich folks are getting away with murder.

Trivial folks only complain about that when the
accused looks like you and me.

Trivial how now they know
they got innocent bruthas on death row
but still got no intentions of letting them go.
Welfare goes up
welfare goes down.
lights on top cop cars in front my house
go round and round. Trivial.

IV.

This life so trivial
compared to the next
with pearly gates, streets of gold
Saint Peter holding transcripts of every lie I told
but here surrounded by trivia
is where I stay
playing games of trivial pursuit every single day
must make my life via trivial means
but shall not base this life on trivial things.

I can fight to remember
whowhenwherewhat   and   why
I am
to keep from going insane

because trivial
this life is
and trivial it must remain.

Street Cipher

/streetci pher
   street ci pher
street cipher/

I am in search of cipher's mystical rays
through this haze and craze
while some folks for days
sing
empty praises to Ned the Wino
But what they don't know is
Ned ain't drunk!
He just acts that way
hoping you'll catch what his cipher has to say
less you dismiss his wisdom, product of that reefer
would rather listen to preacher
with less soul than the concrete beneath my feet
as I pound this pavement in search of my

/streetci pher
   street ci pher
street cipher/

Seinfeld gets more play than the news
you wanna know why our kids abuse
the word?
Baby, that question, absurd
have you not heard what they hear on the radio
You got to be dirty to be down.
Black kings and queens no longer wear crowns.
Now we wear
beepers.
This mess gets deeper and deeper and

deeper into their subconscious
fooling them into thinking
every hip-hop artist is a street philosopher but
they just don't know.
Pray they grow   find their

/streetci pher
    street ci pher
street cipher/

The street   siphons the blood from my veins
siphons the money from my pockets
but you cannot siphon this
what you really want ain't it?
no, you cannot siphon that
what you really need isn't it?
You cannot scoop black woman's essence
with the shovel you gave us to bury our men with
we're using it as a spoon to feed history to babies.
You cannot unlock mysteries of black woman's mind
with the key your great-grandfather
— her slave master —
gave you
that was a dummy room.
Wake, people!
You will never sneak grab   Mother Earth's

/streetci pher
    street ci pher
street cipher/

Street   sounds
will lead you to your cipher
if you know how to listen.
Street   beats
will lead you to ever talkative urban drum

if you know how to   dance
but street signs lead you nowhere
though everywhere
they were not put there by us.
   signs of the times
   signs of our demise
   signs of our crack addiction
   signs of our premature-pregnancy having affliction
   signs of the moms and dads we're disrespecting
None of these signs
have ever been good at reflecting
who we are, who we were
who we are destined to be.
If you want to know what's out there
close those two eyes, use your spare
then you will find   your

/streetci pher
   street ci pher
street cipher/

I am   in search of my cipher
mystical rays through all haze and craze
while some folks for days
sing
empty praises to Ned the Wino
but they don't know
Ned ain't drunk!
He just acts that way
hoping you will catch what his cipher has to say.

Grandma Get Your Gun

Grandma, get your gun.
The wolves are in the yard.
They have come for the children.

You ain't really got to shoot at nobody
just aim for the moon
graze Alpha Centauri's shoulder
let stardust rain down
knock the devil on his ass
make him think twice
bout comin roun' here so quick
soooo slick.
No more.

Grandma, get your gun.
The wolves are in the yard.
It's feeding time.

Destiny is a delicacy
promise quite tasty and
legacy will stick sweet to your ribs
like family reunion barbecue.
Revolution can be a bit lumpy
but goes down smooth like your mashed potatoes.
Grandma, get your gun.

Used to be safe out here in the country.
Young kings and queens could run through the fields
sniffing daffodils
but now the daffodils have been replaced
by snap dragons
breathing down their necks

fires of hellish existence burning away
memories of how to be royalty.
At every corner a new definition of Venus
flytrapping the children's souls
swallowing their consciousness whole
convincing them the natural state of their spirit
is not beautiful.

New-age roosters have turned the babies into
forgetful farm foul.
Coops are filled to overflow
with eagles
thinking that the life of a chicken is acceptable
that flying is overrated.
The weasel has become bold and
the fox fearless
they'll come up over around the fence
into the yard in broad daylight
to snatch your eggs.

Someone taught the jackal how to play the drum.
Now he's tap tap tap tap tapping to the beat
tap tap tap tap tapping to the beat
has mastered the boom-bip.
Watch the children form a line behind him
shaking their groove-thang.
He'll dance them out of the village.

Grandma, the piper's price is too high.
Just shoot him.

I know we hid the guns
to protect the babies
but now the sisters are being
prostituted by hair dye
pimped with fashion.

I know we hid the guns
to protect the babies from misogyny
    misandry, misanthropy
but now brothers don't know
how to defend themselves.
Swapping chains for puppet strings
watch them knock each other out.

Grandma, get your gun shove it down throats
Make them eat their words.
Make them stop eating us for breakfast.

Grandma, get your gun.
Get the buckshot, the hollow-point bullets.
Grandma, get the camouflage.
It is time to stop playing
because life was never a game
freedom never will be and
our survival never is.

Grandma, get your gun.
wolves are in the yard
Grandma, get your gun.
wolves are in the yard
Grandma, Grandma
get your gun
and give it to me.

Swing a language they will all understand.
Swing a song to which we can all dance...
SWING UNIVERSAL

"Those who play the game do not see it as clearly as those who
watch"--*Chinese Proverb*

Synthetic Ulcers

— as if —
climbing rocks wasn't dumb enough
now they got a sport where they jump from 'em
with rubber bands tied to toes
God only knows where
drag racing came from.

When all is said and done
We got too many stupid beer commercials about
frogs lizards some dude named Dick
seven hundred varieties of tummy tucks butt push-ups
breast enlargement breast reduction
lead me to the conclusion

White Folks
ain't got enough problems.

Soon as British ones run out of kids to abuse
American ones start making up the news
exploding airways with tales of my demise due to
black bullets black crack
miss the fact
number one killer of my people is
stress.

— do you know —
It's easier for a white man to rob a bank
than for me to get my own money
out my own bank
from the same teller that deposited my paycheck
    five days before.

Let me tell you my adventures
going to the store.
Don't even check signatures
of strange-looking girl in front of me
charging one hundred and fifty dollars worth
    of nail polish.
Wonder why I look so stylish
when I shop at Macy's?
Wishful maybes
they won't hold my dollar bill upside down
up to the light
before ringing up this blouse
that obviously goes with the suit I got on.

— please come on —
Even buying a pack of gum from Pakistanis
    at 7-Eleven is too hard
wanna see my
driverslicenseregistrationbirthcertificatesocialsecuritycard.

New Age yuppies exhausted limits of
roller blading up down Grand Canyon
bunjy jumping from satellites
can't wait to see what's next.

The most popular sport for middle-class black folk:
leave your home state
try to write a check.

How's a black man
    supposed to come up with a new sport
when he's still trying to come up with excuses
for that new coupe he just bought?
Pulled over by county cops
tobacco jaws swollen
swearing the car is stolen

Dis don look like no nigger-mobile to me.
you shows yous tellin' da truf, boy?

— meanwhile —
NRA finds time to halt legislation
meant to curtail use of favorite twelve gauge toy

Playing chess against computer loses appeal
when you spend all day trying to beat the system.
Shooting stars give rise to fanciful thinking
damn! I must've missed 'em.
Miscellaneous minds create apocalyptic scenarios
just so Hollywood can solve them.
I'm telling y'all

White folks
ain't got enough problems.

Most Black folks probably wish an asteroid would hit
blow this shit
up
So we could start over.
Ever wondered why we name dogs Killa
not Rover?

Over the river and through the woods
but Grandma lives with us
our mathematical fuss is deep
one plus one equals two bedrooms
so where
momdadtwobrothersandsistersauntandgrandma
    gon sleep?

The square root of nothing is nothing
to ghetto kids
higher math seems kind of odd

especially when waiting for big brother to find a job.
Mom's praying you can bet
yet they expect four-year delay
for possibility of bigger paycheck?
Possibility that the fall of affirmative action
is steadily diminishin.

Seems they still have more time
make more movies
about slavery
when maybe
we're still living it.

Go through life
risk it
get that ultimate high
while this country falls apart by and by.
Guilty conscience appeased with fat donations
to poor bloated kids
in countries you've never heard of —
sign that check with pride.

All the while African-American neighbors are dying
on the inside.

Maybe one day white folks will take off those blinders
lower those rose-tinted glasses
finally just
get it
but until then
those self-inflicted ulcers will simply be
synthetic.

Say What

Say what?
Say it white man
with your sights set on affirmative action
you firmly believe in
as long as your wife doesn't make as much money
as you do.

Say what?
Say it again white man
double-forked tongue ready to defend affirmative
action
as long as those Negroes don't take the place
where your son should go
after all junior needs that higher education
to learn quips and etiquette about fraternization
the liquor-golf relationship to success.
Black folk only need that to survive
hell! with a Ph.D. sistah can barely stay alive.
Since we ain't using our diplomas on the green to tee-off
ain't no need for the Missus to get ticked-off
cuz this time old money couldn't buy junior's way
into college
oh yeah, there's a price on the head of knowledge.
What's the point of four generations of Harvard grads
if the great-great-great granddummy can't get in
just cuz he's named after his dad?

Say what?
say say say what you feel...
don't expect me to hear you
you talk that talk I'm not listening
I'm watching

forget Big Brother
check Queen Mother
binding your two faces into one
making your double-talk as apparent as
monumentally coptic shadows in the Set - ting sun.

Say What?
Say who is that?
rather who was that
before he said what he had to say
to get rears in gear to put him in office here.
Now bruh-man got a gubment job
real odd he's nominating covert Klansmen top cop
in a city sixty percent not
what the Aryan nation would like
hope all those little Negroes and Negrettes grow up
be like Mike
cuz despite another negative annual yield
people's good government footin' the bill
for another football field.
Playing sports becomes real cool
when hotel perks shut down another school

Say what?
Say how come
elementary-aged kids with guns not a problem
as long as big crack dealer's children on the corner
shooting each other all day
but big cracker's children totin aussies
in school hallways   is a big deal.
Keep it real:
Ghetto moms and dads see a gun
teach kids to run
redneck moms and dads send kids into the yard with
buckshot to play
while writing checks to the NRA.

Ammunition crossed the color line one way
things kept quiet
bullets manifest as equal opportunity offenders
now the country riots.

Say what?
say say say what you need...
don't expect me to give you an inch
let alone the mile you been asking for
caught with yo hands in the cookie jar
keep runnin you won't get far
I'm skippin behind you like Pepe l'Pu
three eyes, baby, I see you

Say what
the hell is that on television?
feels like war
dodging the fall out from weapons of mass confusion
afraid to give birth beneath this mushroom
could cloud even the brightest minds.
Bad enough Hollywood won't let us have anything but
gangsta
comedic
or pointless flicks
but hey! black actors and producers got to have a job.
(y'all know black folk ain't have money to make
Amistad)
So pay seven-fifty be held hostage by big screens
full of new jacks
prostitutes
welfare jigaboos.
Concentration camp tactics apparent
when same images appear on the news
public press conferences reveal nothing
of hidden agendas subliminal warfare tactics
pushing limits of insanity to the brink

44

who the hell convinced the children
you got to be high to think?

Say what?
say say say what you will...
there will be a reckoning and that's a promise.
don't be so quick to dismiss apocalyptic predictions of
Nostradamos
The end is near.
Speaking out both sides of your neck won't prolong it.
In the next great war
your mind is the battlefield
your soul, the prize
keep your eyes on it!

Say what?

I Prayed For More Gun Control And Got Better Background Checks

I.

I was called out of work today
by my son's principal.
I flew across town in a panic
near despair
only to find that woman had yanked my son
    out of class because
he had braids in his hair
    my God, my God
    keep me from knocking this woman to the floor.
    somehow Holy Spirit lead me
    quietly out the front door
but later that evening
on News Channel 4
two young boys in Denver
have assassinated twelve of their classmates.
I don't know who to pray for anymore.

II.

Another white kid bites the dust
society's upper crust is confused
not used to charging these
blonde-haired, blue-eyed criminals
thanks to six o'clock news subliminals.
So they claim the perpetrators are monsters
clearly not their children
then one of those mass murder high school shootings
happens again
to the parents chagrin
this time bombs were being made
in their own basement

but no amazement coming out of the ghettosphere
we watched society hatch them chickens
knew they had to roost somewhere

out there La La Land is singing a new song.
that tune won't last long
though tomorrow's headlines read
New Public Enemy Number One... The NRA
that's just a platform for Election Day.
A couple hundred thousand dollars in political PACs
congressmen tend to let stuff slide
even though this time
they're taking their own babies along for the ride.

III.

Suburban body count rises
folks wanna ask how? why? what? but
you can't throw rocks in glass houses
and expect your children won't get cut.

Lady Liberty becomes society's highest paid slut
as long as those gunslingers pay her bill
she will continue to yank Uncle Sam's chain.

this is a sick, sick game

As the fallout from this political particulating
hits the safest of places
Uncle Sam laughs in our faces
his minions pass a resolution
suggesting the solution:

Better Background Checks.

IV.

But I did some checking on my own   and found

   7 out of 10 of us Americans think that the Black
Panther party has more members than the Ku Klux
Klan and
   7 out of 10 of us Americans think that the Black
Muslims hide more guns than right white militias and
   7 out of 10 of us Americans think that hip hop's
attitude incites more violence than rock music's mania
and so

with our inclinations
negro affiliations
all we'll be checking for.
7 out of 10 gives the political majority moral superiority
adding morbidity to stupidity until
black boys can't wear braids to school
without being accused of gang-related transgression
while black lipstick spiked hair trench coats
in the dead of summer
is nothing but self-expression.

Before we finish prioritizing criteria for this bogus
background check
check into gilded alabaster family trees
cuz I done sees the enemies
they don't wear oversized FUBU jeans   Malcolm X tees
these well-armed juvenile assassins are sporting
Abercrombie caps and Gap khakis.

V.

Half of these first-degree murderers
below the age of reason.
.38 caliber birthday gift marked the dawn
of his killing season
by age 10 has sharp shooter's aim
has learned life is nothing more than a metaphor
for hunting wild game.
A federal judge sentences another child to death
    or worse
believing the evil he displayed is inherent.
Blame the music, the video games, the child himself
but never, never the parent.
America claims that to be a murderer
one must pull the trigger
gives her citizens an excuse not to look in the mirror.

VI.

Raised kids to think Judgement Day is a movie
but take no responsibility
callous self-denial
leaves our babies cold
fiscally tainted gun control measures, ridiculous.

Be bold.

Stop checking backgrounds
start checking souls.
Reason the death of our children
at society's very core:

better background checks are irrelevant
if we don't know what we're checking for.

crazy

i hear voices
but only because the idiots tapping my line don't know
how to shut up when i'm on the phone

i am not home alone

smile into the mirror
when brushing my teeth
no i'm not looking at me
i'm letting the fools behind the one-way glass know
that i know
    that they know
        that i know   they're there
the scary thing is
they don't even care

take a note

it's like my president
who could care less whether or not i vote
"we've come a long way, baby"
since fergusen vs. plessy
thanks to snoop dogg and jesse
we got tens of thousands of us voting
so i'm told
but only four   or five
of us are counted at the polls

if that's the way love goes
does my country even like me

do you see what i see

my computer shuts down but
never   really   goes off line
              (i know because)
because when i turn it back on
it still knows the time
could those   speakers   that push sound out
really be there to take my sounds back in

think again
with my pen again
a note again and then
try not to hollar   but
it's just like my tax dollar
i know just where the money comes out of
but i don't know what it goes into
       do you?

sam says trust him
it's true
hollywood does too but
i am not impressed with fictional white boys
who see dead people
i see the walking dead every day
through bmore chi-town hotlanta
young men morph into maggots
eat the big apple from the inside out
there's no question what this vision is about
hysteria? runscreamshout:

       chicken little was clairvoyant
       all hail little boy blue and that damned horn

if insanity is what's different   from the norm
what happens
when all the normal people are crazy

Swing love through everything. Swing love for everything. Swing love because it is everything…
SWING LOVE

IV

"Love, and do whatever else you like"--*Saint Augustine*

Some Poetry

I went into the city
and met some poetry
so sweet
he melts in your mouth
if you can work up the nerve to say his name.
I went into the city
and met some poetry
not the caramel they talk about
not the mocha chocolate black cinnamon sprinkled
coffee they write songs for
not that fine fresh blueberry dark we dream of
he was his own shade of paradise
and now I'm humming his song.

It wasn't just that he sang
he made music out of nothing
melody out of madness
turned rain into rhythm unheard of and familiar
in one breath.

I dreamed of him last night
we were walking along the beach
playing tag with the ocean
getting dance lessons from the waves
knew I couldn't go underwater
knew I'd forget to breathe
find myself tongue-kissing starfish
and I had something, someone else in mind
some poetry on my mind.
I was so busy inhaling him
couldn't worry about things as irrelevant
as air

Going back to the suburbs now
wayward Queen Bee
returning to the hive
but I'm taking some poetry with me.
He penetrated my skin
like shea butter after a bath
stayed on my lips
as thick as hips
as forever as pyramids
as unforgettable as Some good poetry.

He was not the caramel they talk about
not the mocha chocolate black cinnamon sprinkled
coffee they write songs for
not that fine fresh blueberry dark we dream of
he was his own shade of paradise

and now I'm humming his song.

Could I Move You

If I wrapped myself around you
like an East Wind
cool in the Fall, hot in the Spring
blew and blew the fury of monsoons
blew and blew swelling tides like the moon
Could I move you?

If I beat through you
a talking drum
pulsating in your veins as my own
beating and beating over the rhythm of your heart
beating and beating, no stop no start
Could I move you?

If I built myself around you
an archive of Timbuktu
preserving your grace, framing your beauty
the stone of my walls to house your essence
the stone of my walls your temple, eternal blessing
Could I move you?

If I burned in you
like the Nairobi Sun
fire flaming in your spirit, in your soul
my heart warming you all the night through
my heart warming the hearth you come home to
Could I move you?

I ask   because
you move   me.

W.A.R.

(Worshiping.A.Revolutionary)
Mmmm

I just love me a soldier

See
Looking for that revolutionary
I was meant to marry because
He was mine in my
Last two lifetimes

I've always been partner
To a warrior

My first love was Shango
And though
He may not recognize me

I'll know
    Him
By the spear he carries

Come bring the revolution
with me
my revolutionary.

his shirt

i like to cuddle up
late at night
wrap myself in his shirt
two, maybe three sizes too big
reminds me of
cuddling up in his arms that are
two, maybe three sizes just right

warm, soft rivets of cotton
moving, rustling up and down my skin
sort of like the hair on his arms
when he tightens his grip around me
i reach up, pull the collar close
imitate whiskers on his face as he leans in
for a silent sneaky kiss
on my cheek
on my neck
behind my ear

this shirt
warm shirt
maybe two, three sizes too big used to be
four maybe five sizes too large
washed and overwashed
worn and overworn
smells like me and not like him anymore
but that's cool because sometimes
after long nights
or even long days
he doesn't smell so much like him anymore
but like me
and that's how i know that he is really mine

60

still his own man
still his shirt
but that doesn't change the fact
we don't call it
the gray shirt
we call it my shirt
and we don't call him his name
we call him my man

when he's gone
i still have his shirt
that's maybe two, three sizes too big
and on the longer nights i wrap myself up in it
cuddling
reminded of his arms around me
two maybe three sizes just right

Until you find yourself, swing swing swing.
And when you find yourself, swing swing
swing. In celebration of yourself,
swing swing swing...

SWING SWING SWING

V

"When I discover myself, I'll be free"*--**Ralph Ellison**

the untitled SUPERHERO poem

I have SUPERPOWERS
Yes. Yes, I do

Faster than lazy welfare house hoes
more powerful than non-voting Negroes
able to relate to unsuspecting White Folk in a single
conversation

I am SUPERWOMAN

By day…
mild-mannered exception to that rule
but once on city streets
I blend into urban blocks like mailbox
13-year co-workers from the next cubicle
can't see me
INVISIBLE

TELEKINETIC
Now in my human form
can't so much as move a school board to buy school
books for school children
but after 6 o'clock
can move crowds of innocent old white ladies
across streets and down blocks at inhuman speeds
with a single glance

I am that BEAST

Though powers did not manifest until late in life
as a child: acceptable
afro-puffs: adorable   then

the MUTANT GENES kicked in
hips grew to SUPERHUMAN PROPORTIONS
butt enlarged to NATIONAL SECURITY THREAT
hair grew in so nappy   so nappy
(it was   SUPER NATURAL)
that's when arch rival African Pride
started producing perm.
But get this…

I am also SHAPE-SHIFTER

I can walk into a convenience store
6 foot 9 inches black as night bald as day
weigh in at whopping 497 pounds
then leave
and by the time the cops catch me
I am   5'4" light-skinned with Afro
weighing 93 pounds   wet

Out of my homeland
where I was just an ordinary princess
abilities grew beyond imagination
vowed to use SUPERHUMAN STRENGTHS
to save my adopted homeworld
from the horrors of
whatever
so they would love me like SUPERMAN
but instead
they treat me like   the WONDER TWINS

pointless
powerless
and wondering   why
they ever brought me on the show
in the first place.

Nothing to Wear

I'm supposed to be trodding footsteps of
    past-time queens
but I can't in these dull, flat things
gave away gold-toed high-steppin high heels of Shaka
 Zulu's mamma
sold 7-inch stilettos Cleopatra wore to make the
 Romans look up to her Sun
put out platforms I used to use to remind then Yoruba
 why they called me the moon.

I swear I'll recreate my wardrobe soon.

This ensemble is just disguise
to help me blend and camouflage into their lies
— I mean lives —
not mine
but in the meantime
put on that new dress
two sizes too small for my spirit and
clearly the wrong color for my soul tone
but flattened thighs and squished hips
made my ancestors look like they'd spent less time in
 the sun
figured it'd get the job done
after all I did have that interview.

But I became the vampire

desperately sucking blood from my life force
until my frame of self-reference was drained enough to
squeeze into these pants
on top of this girdle

on top of these push-up panties
— designed for them by them —
make my rear end look more flat
like my nose used to be
before swapping it for one that matched my power
suits
camouflaged my roots appropriately
to better hear the jangle of shackles piercing my ear
drowning out drumbeats that used to be near enough
to dance to.

Turned my head
got a clearer view of suburban greens
convinced those ends would justify these means
made vow to become living proof
That alter egos can exist under one roof
but who would win

the war inside me?
Not a battle without casualty

carcasses of slaughtered value systems lay as far as the
 eye could see
sweaters that brought out the Soweto in my eyes
 were dying
skirts that swung with the defiance in my hips were
 already dead
blouses that blossomed with memories of nations
 suckling at my bosom
were summarily sentenced and hung.
Songs of pride no longer sung by fisted earrings and
cartouche pendants
changed from black gold to fool's gold
ancestral alchemy undone.

I burned incense in my closet

to cover the stench of dead dreams and
rotting self-images
surrounded by clouds of burning sandalwood
looked more like myself than I had in ages
but when the smoke cleared
I was still blind to the permanence of these temporary
wardrobe changes
— a belt for Mr. Charlie —
— a suit is for his wife —
picking personas to please
became substance of my life
then   yesterday
I got promoted
finally I would be HNIC
could put on anything my spirit pointed out to me
be rid of these All-American Girl Blues
could put on clothes as Black
— as African —
as I choose
could even lace cowry shells through my hair
but forced to look in that same old closet
I found I had nothing to wear.

Double Consciousness

I.
southern trees bear strange fruit

...but let me tell you bout them Manhattan maples
dropping crooked cops on police academy lawns
like heavy leaves in fall
heavy leaves in fall
like heavy tears for all seasons.

Without reasons
ghetto law enforcement officials feel they can
reload their clips
when chasing a single, unarmed black man
reinvention of the lynchin
as effective as it was back then.

Joseph Palcinsky killed 4 people took 3 hostages
and it was 13 days before police even shot at him.

society bears no truth
tell me what's really going on

II.
…and every black revolutionary
has written a Diallo poem
as well they shoulda
coulda. Would I knew
why my dear Amadu was even carrying a wallet.
Extra Africans in America not supposed to have
no money
just criminal records
and matching intent.
All the time we've spent trying to convince the Po-Po
shootin innocent black folks is a no-no
why don't we just shoot back?
shoot first in fact

…except that
my first accident, my fault.
Everybody yelling and screaming
why didn't you stop?
The first person to say
How you doing?
was a cop.
All the concerned citizens
    more concerned with being on TV
the next person to show any more concern for me
was another cop.

my dad.

III.
Wish I had a nickel
hell, a penny would be plenty
for every stop sign we really didn't run
for every jury that said
what they did was what had to be done
for every district attorney we did not vote for
and what's more
a little change for all the laws that didn't.
Wouldn't I be a rich woman?
But green money don't protect colored people
in the land of red, white and blue
where Uncle Sam wants you
out of the family photographs.

Unconvicted murderers share back-alley laughs
but clearly we who are angry
now out number the coppuhs
so what's to stop us from
taking them all out
in grand revolutionary act...

...except that
there's the little white boy down the street
I baby-sit every week
has Scruff McGruff the Crime Dog posters
every release
pretty sure that child gon grow and be the police

but throughout my revolutionary din
I have not heard one sound that will spare him.

IV.
oh, but Sodom
is righteously condemned
the bible sayeth so
(except that)
God said if there be but one good person
he'd let them go
and I just gave me three
we folks have been so wronged
we can justify World War III
(except that)
we folks have been here so long
we can no longer recognize the enemy.

V.
...no brutality in Philly
cuz that time the bruthas were in on it, too.
dat wat happen when ya attack da messenger
let da message fly right by you

...not simply
defending capitalism's conspiring whores
counter-revolutionizing freedom wars
when we let them to close doors
to closets filled with our bones.

There be Pyric victory in eliminating *them*
killing too many of our own.
...no good in attacking symptoms
leave-be the disease.

Time I choose what is necessary.

All this talk about becoming a new revolutionary
when what I need is
a revolutionized attack.

There will be no real live battle plans
if I except that.

Last Will and Testimony

According to Laini Mataka
being a strong black woman
can get you killed
So I stand before you today
with this Last Testimony and Will
because I may be dead soon.
But I can't greet that last moon
with peace of mind until I leave behind
a few things the Son left me.

To my sisters
I leave every single nap
for I own nothing more powerful than that.

To my brothers
I leave these hips.
Little known fact
you can't carry a nation on just your back.

To my children
I leave the words to my favorite freedom song
the melody unspecified.
Melody is your choice
find your own voice.

To my builders
I leave lines from a beloved
James Weldon Johnson poem.
You must build our houses out of more
than rocks and stone.

To my doctor
I leave my priest.
To my priest
I leave my lawyer.
To my lawyer
I leave my mirror.
You can't heal the body
until you heal the soul. You can't heal the soul
until you have the courage to sue the devil
but you can't go after the devil
until you look in the mirror
make sure he's not the one sitting on your back.

And to those who relinquished membership
in the family
I leave the beat.
I want to teach you the rhythm
you are afraid to give me the chance.
Beware: revolution will be sounded by the drum.
Your only hope is to remember
the dance.

Acknowledgments

This – like everything else we do of import – was not a solo project. There are many people who helped me and inspired me. Thank you all....

...especially you, Mommy – more than a mom, an editor, a sounding board, office supply company... cook. Thank you Grandmommy, my ad hoc copyeditor. You could find a needle in a haystack. Thank you Kwame and Stephanie – of course, this is your baby, too!

...especially all of you who inspired particular poems. You know who you are, but also know how much you have meant to me.

...especially uou, Tif and Uche and Maria and Derrick. You have always kept me in mind and heart. You have supported me in this for love.

...especially you roger you are more than brilliant you are gifted i will forsake punctuation and pretense and organization for you who took the time to teach me why this project is what it is because of who you are...

About the Author

Tonya Maria Matthews is a graduate of Duke University, currently completing her doctorate in biomedical engineering at John's Hopkins University in Maryland. She began writing poetry as a child and branched into play and editorial writing in college. In the fall of 1998 she toured with her performance poetry troupe under her stage name "JaHipster." In 2000, she was selected as a member of the Washington, DC National Slam Team. Her chapbook, "These Hips," was published in 1999, the year she was crowned Inaugural BlackWords Slam Champion. One of nine writers honored throughout 2000 by the Maryland Center for the Book, her work has been featured on Horizonmag.com and the Jazz Poetry Kafe CD, where she appears alongside Haki Madhubuti, Fertile Ground and Sonia Sanchez. Currently, Tonya Maria is working on her spoken word CD set to release in 2002. For more information and to arrange bookings, visit her at www.JaHipster.com.

About the Publisher

Established in 1995, BlackWords, Inc., is a Washington, DC Metropolitan-based Independent Publisher and Producer of fine Black Literature & Performance. The primary mission of the house is to provide opportunities for a new generation of Talented Literary Artists. Since our inception in 1995 we have published eleven works of Literary & Genre Fiction, Poetry and Creative Non-fiction; and produced over 100 poetry, theatre and arts-related events.

Visit us online at **www.BlackWordsonline.com** for more information.